A Kid's Book of Experiments With

COLOR

SURPRISING Science Experiments

Robert Gardner
and
Joshua Conklin

Enslow Publishing
101 W. 23rd Street
Suite 240
New York, NY 10011
USA

enslow.com

Published in 2016 by Enslow Publishing, LLC
101 W. 23rd Street, Suite 240, New York, NY 10011

Library of Congress Cataloging-in-Publication Data

Gardner, Robert, 1929- author.
 A kid's book of experiments with color / Robert Gardner and Joshua Conklin.
    pages cm. — (Surprising science experiments)
 Audience: Ages 9+
 Audience: Grades 4 to 6.
 Summary: "Details science experiments about color with explanations"—
Provided by publisher.
 Includes bibliographical references and index.
 ISBN 978-0-7660-7201-5 (library binding)
 ISBN 978-0-7660-7199-5 (pbk.)
 ISBN 978-0-7660-7200-8 (6-pack)
1. Color—Experiments—Juvenile literature. 2. Light—Experiments—Juvenile
literature. I. Conklin, Joshua, author. II. Title.
 QC495.5.G38 2016
 535.6—dc23

2015029980

Printed in the United States of America

To Our Readers: We have done our best to make sure all website addresses in this book were active and appropriate when we went to press. However, the author and the publisher have no control over and assume no liability for the material available on those websites or on any websites they may link to. Any comments or suggestions can be sent by e-mail to customerservice@enslow.com.

Photo Credits: Throughout book: Wiktoria Pawlak/Shutterstock.com (lightbulbs), Sapann-Design/Shutterstock.com (colorful alphabet), Login/Shutterstock.com (series logo), Aleksandrs Bondars/Shutterstock.com (colorful banners), VLADGRIN/Shutterstock.com (science background), vector-RGB/Shutterstock.com (arrows); cover, p. 1 Master1305/Shutterstock.com (girl doing chemistry experiment); p. 4 ZouZou/Shutterstock.com; p. 6 bogdan ionescu/Shutterstock.com; p. 7 ASchindl/Shutterstock.com; p. 11 Richard Griffin/Shutterstock.com; p. 15 Andreas Liem/Shutterstock.com; p. 18 OlgaLis/Shutterstock.com; p. 19 saga1966/Shutterstock.com; p. 30 Take Photo/Shutterstock.com; p. 44 Laurin Rinder/Shutterstock.com.

Illustration Credits: Accurate Art, Inc. c/o George Barile

CONTENTS

Introduction

Colors are one of the first things a child is taught. You learn from a young age that "green means go and red means stop" and that an apple can be either of these colors. You pick a favorite color (or two) and make bright pictures to hang on the wall. But how much do you really know about color? In this book, you will explore and learn about colors by conducting a series of experiments. From the beauty of a rainbow to the beauty of an artist's brushstroke, you will discover how colors interact with your world. Let's get started!

Sunlight: Prisms and Rainbows

If you were asked to draw the sun, what color would you choose? Yellow? Orange? Or perhaps, if it is setting, red? While you might find the perfect crayon to represent the sun in your picture, what is the color of the light coming from the sun? Let's conduct some experiments to find out.

Experiment 1: The Colors in Sunlight

Things You Will Need:

- sun
- water hose with spray nozzle
- glass or plastic prism
- white wall

Sir Isaac Newton was one of the world's greatest scientists and mathematicians. He helped make a number of important scientific discoveries. He was also the first to demonstrate the colors in sunlight. Now we can show the same thing.

1. On a sunny day, find a hose with a spray nozzle.
2. Stand with your back to the sun.
3. Spray water in front of you until you see a rainbow in the sprayed drops. What colors can you see?
4. Hold a glass or plastic prism in sunlight near a white wall. **(Don't look at the sun. It can damage your eyes!)**
5. Slowly turn the prism until you see a spectrum (a band of colors) on the wall.

   What colors do you see? Are they the colors you saw in the rainbow you made with the hose?

You need both sun and rain to see a rainbow.

Blow some soap bubbles like these. You will see tiny rainbows of color in the bubbles.

Experiment 2:
A Lightbulb and a Prism

Like Sir Isaac Newton himself, you proved that the light from the sun is composed of a spectrum of colors. Now you can prove something even Newton didn't have a chance to discover. What color is the light coming from a lightbulb? Let's find out.

Things You Will Need:

- heavy black construction paper
- scissors
- clear lightbulb with a small filament or a clear tubular showcase bulb with one long vertical filament

1. Have **an adult** place either a clear lightbulb with a small filament or a clear tubular bulb with a single straight filament into a socket or lamp fixture. (Figure 1c).

2. Find a sheet of heavy black construction paper and cut a rectangle that is about 10 cm x 15 cm (4 in x 6 in).

3. Find the center of one long side of the rectangle and carefully cut a narrow (1 mm wide) vertical slit about 6 cm (2.5 in) long.

Figure 1

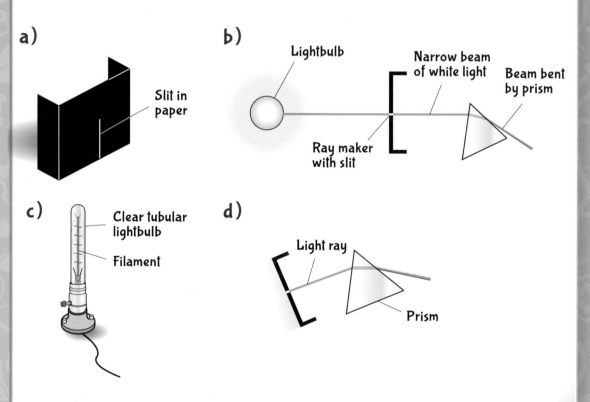

a)

Slit in paper

b)

Lightbulb

Narrow beam of white light

Beam bent by prism

Ray maker with slit

c)

Clear tubular lightbulb

Filament

d)

Light ray

Prism

a) Make a black standup "ray maker." A narrow slit will let a beam of light pass through. b) This view of the experiment is seen from above. c) A clear tubular lightbulb has a straight line filament. d) The light ray is bent both entering and leaving the prism.

4. Fold about 3.5 cm (1.5 in) of the paper at each end so it will stand upright. See Figure 1a.

5. In a room that can be made dark, set up the experiment as shown in Figure 1b. The lightbulb should be about 30 cm (1 ft) from the black upright paper.

6. Make the room dark and turn on the light. A narrow beam (ray) of light will come through the slit.

7. Place the prism on the narrow light beam. Turn the prism so the light ray hits the prism at an angle. The narrow light beam will bend as it enters and leaves the prism (Figure 1d).

8. Slowly and carefully turn the prism. Make the light bend more and more. Do colors begin to appear? If they do, which color is bent the most? Which color is bent the least?

Sunlight Has Many Colors: An Explanation

When you made a rainbow with sunlight using the hose or prism you probably saw violet, blue, green, yellow, orange, and red. Rainbows are made when rays of sunlight enter water droplets. The rays are bent, reflected, and bent again when they exit the water droplets. Some colors bend more than others and this separates them into a rainbow.

As you discovered, the same rainbow of colors comes from a lightbulb. You hopefully saw that violet was bent the most and red was bent the least. Nice job following in the footsteps and expanding on the work of Sir Isaac Newton!

A prism can separate white light into the colors it contains.

Mixing Colored Lights

You learned in the previous chapter that both sunlight and artificial light (lightbulbs) contain all the colors of the rainbow. You also probably know how to add and subtract. So what happens when you mix (add together) various colors of light? Let's do an experiment to find out.

Experiment 3: Mixing (Adding) Colors

Things You Will Need:

- an adult
- 3 light sockets
- red, blue, and green light bulb
- white wall
- dark room
- cardboard sheet about 30 cm x 45 cm (12 in x 18 in)

1. Have **an adult** put three light sockets with red, blue, and green lightbulbs near a white wall in a room that can be made dark (see Figure 2).

Figure 2

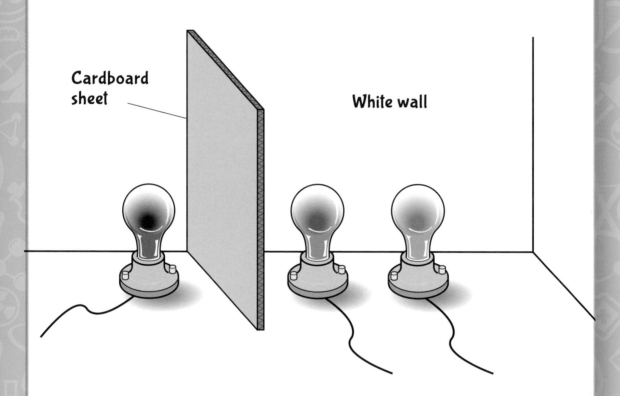

Cardboard sheet

White wall

Three colored light bulbs (red, blue, and green) are placed near a white wall in a dark room. The different colors can be mixed by moving the cardboard.

Leave a space of about 5 cm (2 in) between the sockets. Put the bulbs about 20 cm (8 in) from the wall.

2. **Ask an adult** to plug in the red and blue lights. Make the room dark except for these two lights.

3. Hold a cardboard sheet against the wall and between the two lit bulbs (Figure 2). Pull the cardboard back several centimeters. This will let the two colors overlap and mix on the wall. What color do you see when you mix blue and red lights?

4. Mix blue and green lights in the same way. What color do you see when you mix blue and green?

5. Mix red and green lights. What color do you see? Did the color surprise you?

6. Turn on all three lights. Hold the cardboard sheet between the red and blue bulbs and against the wall. Pull the cardboard back a tiny bit. You will see the red and green lights mix. Pull it farther back a little more until all three colors can mix. What color results when all three colors are added together?

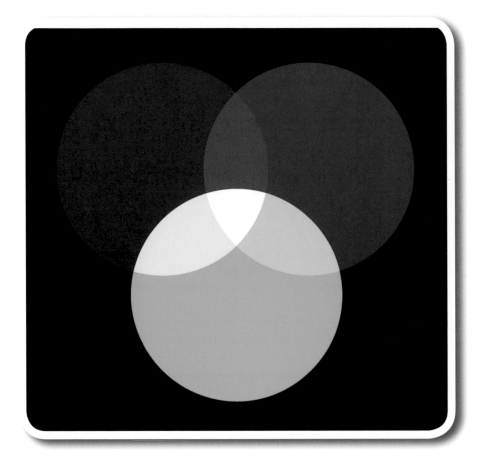

The photo shows how the primary colors of light combine to make cyan, magenta, and yellow.

Figure 3

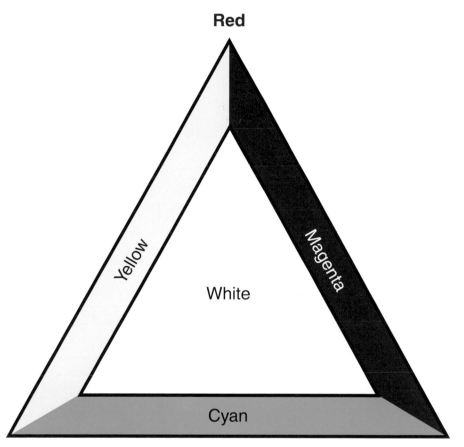

This is a color triangle. The primary colors of light (red, green, and blue) are at the corners of the triangle. The complementary colors are along the opposite side of the primary color's corner. For example, green is a primary color. Its complementary color is magenta. When added together, a primary color and its complementary color produce white light.

Mixing Colored Lights: An Explanation

If you have ever mixed paints, the colors you got when mixing lights probably surprised you. A mix of blue and red light makes magenta, which you might call pink. Mixing blue and green light makes cyan, which you might call blue-green or aqua. Adding red and green light together makes yellow.

Mixing all three lights produced white. Because red, blue, and green light combine to form white light, they are called the primary colors of light.

A colored light that combines with a primary color to make white light is called a complementary color. The color triangle in Figure 3 shows how this works. Cyan is a mix of green and blue light, so added to red light, the result is white light. The same result occurs when adding blue and yellow (red + green) and green and magenta (blue + red). In all three examples, the three primary colors of light are added together.

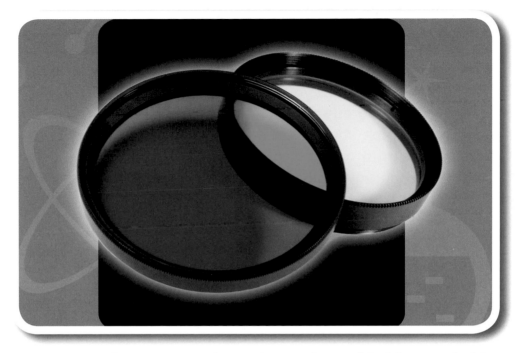

You can also mix complementary colors of light using light filters. A mix of yellow and cyan lights will produce green.

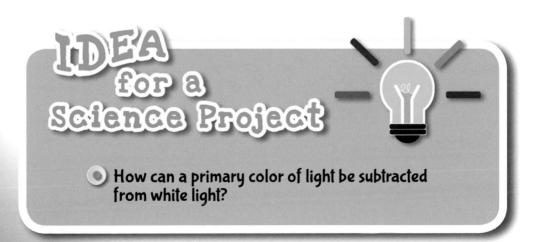

IDEA for a Science Project

- How can a primary color of light be subtracted from white light?

Colored Shadows

On a sunny day your shadow never leaves your side. The shadow is dark because you are an opaque object (you block the light). The sunlight can't reach the ground, creating a dark spot. But what would happen if some colored light shined on a dark shadow?

If you've ever been out walking in the snow on a bright blue day, you may have noticed that your shadow appeared blue too. A shadow on snow is one place you can find colored shadows. In the next experiment, you'll learn more about how colored shadows are made.

What do you think makes this shadow blue?

Experiment 4:
Adding Color to Shadows

Things You Will Need:

- an adult
- 3 light sockets and bulbs from Experiment 3
- white wall
- dark room
- clay
- pencil

1. **Ask an adult** to insert a red, blue, and green lightbulb into three light sockets.

2. Put the sockets about 30 cm (12 in) in front of a white wall in a room that can be made dark. Leave a space of about 5 cm (2 in) between the sockets (Figure 4).

3. **Ask an adult** to plug in the blue light.

4. Using a lump of clay, place a pencil upright about 8 cm (3 in) from the wall. Put it in front of the blue light. Is the pencil's shadow dark?

5. Is it dark if you use only the red or green light?

6. Put the pencil close to the wall between the blue and green lights. Predict the number of shadows you will see when both the blue and green lights are on.

Figure 4

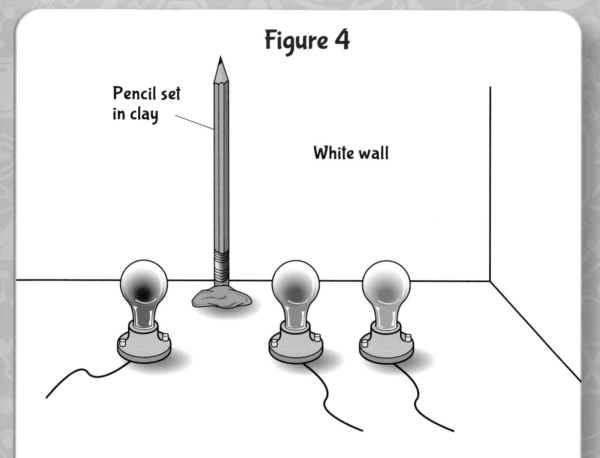

Pencil set in clay

White wall

What colors are the shadows cast by colored lights?

7. Turn on both the green and blue lights. Was your prediction correct? How do you explain the color of the shadows?

8. Repeat the experiment using the red and green lights. How many shadows do you see? How do you explain the color of the shadows?

9. Repeat the experiment using the red and blue lights. How many shadows do you see? How do you explain the color of the shadows?

10. Repeat the experiment with all three lights turned on, placing the pencil in the middle. How many shadows do you see? How do you explain the color of the shadows?

Colored Shadows: An Explanation

A dark shadow can be colored by a second light source. Your normally dark shadow appears blue in the snow because the bright white snow reflects blue light from the sky.

If two lights shine on an object, it casts two shadows. The blue light cast a shadow on the wall and that shadow is colored by the green light (making the shadow green). Similarly the blue light colored the shadow cast by the green light. The same thing occurred with the other combinations of two different colored lights. See Figures 5a, 5b, and 5c.

With three lights on, there were three shadows (Figure 5d). Their colors may have surprised you. Two lights, red and green, shone on the shadow cast by the blue light. Since red light added to green light makes yellow, that shadow was yellow. The shadow cast by the green light was colored by blue and red light. Since blue and red light added together make magenta, that shadow was magenta. Since blue and green light shone on the shadow caused by the red light, its color was cyan.

Who knew shadows could come in so many colors!

Figure 5

a)

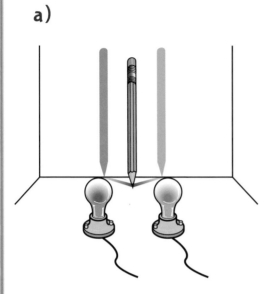

b)

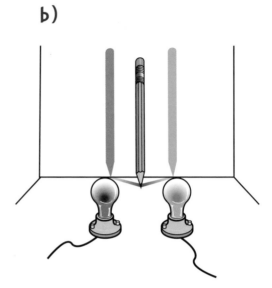

c)

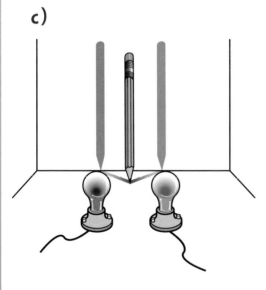

d)

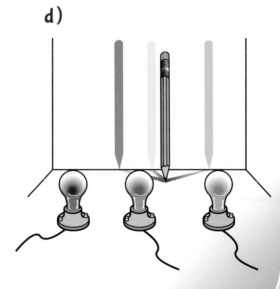

Can you explain the color of the shadows cast by these colored lights?

IDEA
for a
Science Project

- Look for colored shadows in the world around you and look for an explanation. For example, shadows seen on snow are often blue. Shadows around a Christmas tree lit with multicolored bulbs may have many colors.

Colors and Afterimages

Have you ever closed your eyes after staring off into space (we are sure you were not daydreaming during school or while your parents were talking . . .) and seen an image that seems to float on your closed eyelids? You had probably been staring at a light and the "floaty thing" that appeared after you closed your eyes is called an afterimage. You can create one right now by staring at a bright lightbulb for a few seconds and then closing your eyes and counting to ten. The image of the bulb remains on the retina (back of your eye) but it has a different color! To see how afterimages are affected by color, let's do an experiment.

Experiment 5: Primary Colors and Afterimages

Things You Will Need:

- blue, green, and red construction paper
- scissors
- ruler
- 2 sheets of white paper
- chair
- a table or counter

1. Cut out 8 cm x 8 cm (3 in x 3 in) squares of blue, green, and red construction paper. (Remember blue, green, and red are the primary colors of light.)

2. Place two sheets of white paper side by side on a table.

3. Put your blue square on one sheet of paper. Stare at the blue square for about fifteen seconds.

4. After you have stared at the colored square, shift your gaze to the other sheet of white paper. After a second or two, you should see an afterimage. What color is the afterimage?

5. Repeat the experiment twice. First use the green square and then use the red. What color is the afterimage when using green? When using red?

According to one theory of color vision, we have three types of cone cells around the center of our retinas. These cells are responsible for how we see color. One kind of cone cell responds only to red light, another only to green light, and a third only to blue light.

Using this theory, try to explain the afterimages you saw when doing this experiment.

○ What color afterimage would you expect to see after staring at a black square, a lemon, or an orange?

Experiment 6:
Complementary Colors and Afterimages

Things You Will Need:

- ● cyan, magenta, and yellow construction paper
- ◉ scissors
- ◉ hammer
- ● 2 sheets of white paper
- ● a table or counter

You have seen the afterimages that primary colors create. A colored light that combines with a primary color to make white light is called a complementary color. (Look again at Figure 3.) The complementary colors are cyan, magenta, and yellow. Try to predict the color of the afterimages you will see after you stare at cyan, magenta, and yellow squares.

1. Cut out 8 cm x 8 cm (3 in x 3 in) squares of cyan, magenta, and yellow construction paper.

2. Place two sheets of white paper side by side on a table.

3. Put a cyan square on one sheet of paper. Stare at the cyan square for about fifteen seconds.

4. After you have stared at the colored square, shift your gaze to the other sheet of white paper. After a second or two, you should see a bright afterimage. What color is the afterimage?

5. Repeat the experiment using the magenta and yellow squares separately. What color is the afterimage when using magenta? When using yellow?

Were you able to predict the colors of the afterimages?

Colors and Afterimages: An Explanation

If you use the same muscle over and over again the muscle will eventually tire and need rest. The same thing happens to the cone cells inside your eyes.

When you stared at a red square, the cells that respond to that color tired. Then you switched your gaze to a white sheet of paper and all three types of cone cells (red, green, and blue) tried to respond. However, the weary red-sensitive cone cells didn't respond as well as the rested green and blue cone cells. Since blue and green combine to make cyan, you saw a cyan afterimage. For similar reasons, you saw a magenta afterimage after staring at a green square and a yellow afterimage after staring at a blue square.

When you stared at a cyan square, the cone cells that respond to green and blue tired (remember cyan is a combination of green and blue). When you turned your gaze to a white sheet, all three types of cone cells were stimulated. However, the tired green and blue cone cells did not respond as well as the rested red cone cells. So this time you saw a red afterimage. And after staring at a yellow square you saw a blue afterimage and a green afterimage when you stared at a magenta square.

IDEA for a Science Project

- Can you mix colored lights using afterimages?

Colors in Colored Light

Have you ever been walking down a street at night lit with street lamps and noticed how things appear slightly different? This is because street lamps are often mercury vapor lights, which can give off a yellow or green glow. To see how colored lights change the way things look, try this next experiment.

How might the color of these lights change the way things look?

Experiment 7: How Colored Light Changes What We See

Things You Will Need:

- an adult
- light socket
- red, green, and blue lightbulbs
- very dark room
- white, black, red, green, yellow, and blue construction paper

1. Place a light socket with a red lightbulb near a white wall in a room that can be made dark. **Ask an adult** to connect the socket to an electrical outlet.

2. Cut out 5 cm x 5 cm (2 in x 2 in) squares of white, black, red, yellow, green, and blue construction paper.

3. Make the room dark and turn on only the red bulb. Hold the white paper square in the red light. What color does the white paper have in red light?

4. Repeat the experiment using black, red, yellow, green, and blue paper. What color does each colored square have in red light? Write down your results.

5. **Ask the adult** to replace the red lightbulb with a blue lightbulb. Repeat the experiment again for each colored square. Write down your results.

6. **Ask the adult** to replace the blue lightbulb with a green lightbulb. Then repeat the experiment for each piece of colored paper. Write down your results.

Colors in Colored Light: An Explanation

A red object remains red in red light because it reflects the red light. The red dyes in a red object absorb all colors *except* red. The same is true of blue and green objects. They reflect only blue or green light. They absorb light of all other colors. Yellow, as you learned in Experiment 3, is a mixture of green and red light. Yellow objects reflect both green and red light.

A white object reflects all light. If only red light shines on it, it will appear red. In blue light it will appear to be blue, and so on. A black object absorbs light of all colors, so it looks dark in light of any color.

Blue objects appear dark in red and green light because they absorb red and green light. The same is true of green objects in red and blue light. It is also true of red objects in blue and green light.

Your results may be different. For example, the blue paper may have looked green in green light. This happens if the blue paper reflects some green light as well as blue. Any object that contains dyes other than its basic color will reflect some of those other colors.

IDEAS for a Science Project

- Obtain transparent pieces of plastic that have different colors. Predict what colors you will see when you look at them in light of different colors.

- Examine a color painting in several different colored lights. How does it change the painting?

Subtracting Colors

You have seen that light of different colors can be added (mixed) together. Let's look at another kind of color arithmetic. Is it possible to subtract colored light?

Experiment 8: Subtracting Colors Using Colored Filters

Things You Will Need:

- an adult
- lamp or light socket
- clear tubular showcase lightbulb with a single straight filament
- diffraction grating (from science teacher, science catalog, or hobby store)
- colored plastic or cellophane light filters with colors of red, green, blue, magenta, yellow, and cyan

1. **Ask an adult** to plug a lamp or light socket into an electrical outlet and add a lightbulb. The lightbulb should be a clear tubular showcase lightbulb with a long single straight filament (see Figure 1c).

2. Hold a diffraction grating in front of your eye. The grating has thousands of very narrow slits. When light goes through the slits, it is diffracted (spread out). As you will see, some colors of light are spread more than others. Look at the light coming from the lightbulb through the grating. What do you see? (You may have to turn the grating one-quarter turn if the light is not spread horizontally.)

Longer light waves are diffracted (spread out) more than shorter wavelengths. From what you see, which light color has the longest light waves? Which color has the shortest wavelengths? Which color is in between?

3. You can subtract colors. Hold a piece of colored filter in front of the diffraction grating. Look at the light through the grating and the colored filter (Figure 6). How can you tell if any color has been subtracted?

4. Hold a red filter in front of the grating. What color or colors have been subtracted?

5. In the same way, test a number of colored filters. Try to predict which color, or colors, will be subtracted by green, blue, magenta, yellow, and cyan filters.

6. Suppose you make a "sandwich" of a blue filter and a red filter, what colors do you think will be subtracted? Will any colors remain?

Figure 6

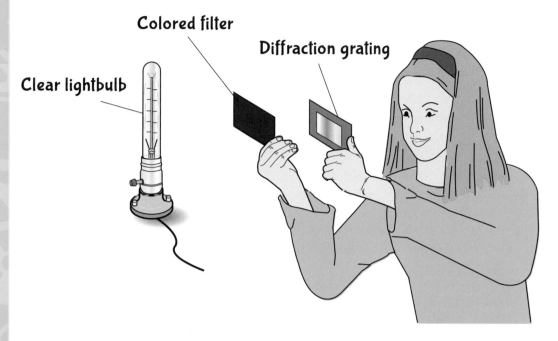

Clear lightbulb

Colored filter

Diffraction grating

Look at the light through a colored filter. Then hold a diffraction grating in front of the filter. What color(s) does the filter remove from the light? What colors does it allow to pass through?

7. Make a chart like the one on page 37. Make the filter sandwiches listed. Test each one, in turn, by holding the "sandwich" in front of the grating. Try to predict which colors, if any, you will see. Then look through the "sandwiches" and the grating. Record your results. The authors recorded their results for the first one (blue + red).

You may find this technique helpful. Look at the white light through the grating. Then move the filter "sandwich" in front of the grating.

How good were your predictions? Don't be disappointed if some of your predictions were not correct. Colored filters vary in quality; some do not subtract all the colors you might expect.

Colors in the Filter Sandwich	Colors I Expect to See	Colors I Saw	Colors in the Filter Sandwich	Colors I Expect to See	Colors I Saw
1. blue + red	none	none	9. green + magenta		
2. blue + green			10. blue + cyan		
3. red + green			11. blue + yellow		
4. red + cyan			12. blue + magenta		
5. red + yellow			13. cyan + magenta		
6. red + magenta			14. cyan + yellow		
7. green + cyan			15. yellow + magenta		
8. green + yellow					

Subtracting Colors Using Colored Filters: An Explanation

So how good were your color subtracting skills? Any filter of a primary color should remove all colors other than the color of the filter. Any sandwich made of two primary colors, such as blue + red, should remove all the colors coming from the white light.

A sandwich of a primary color and its complementary color, such as red + cyan, blue + yellow, or green + magenta should also remove all color.

Subtracting Colored Light Using Pigments (Paint)

Have you ever looked at a beautiful painting full of brilliant colors and wondered how the artist did that? Artists can use the pigments in paints to subtract color.

From what we have already learned you might expect green paint to have only green pigments. Because it is green, it would reflect only green light and absorb the other colors in white light. You might expect the same for other paints and colorings. But is that what happens? You can do an experiment to find out!

Experiment 9: Subtracting Colors Using Pigments in Food Coloring

Things You Will Need:

- an adult
- lamp or light socket
- clear tubular showcase lightbulb with a single straight filament
- diffraction grating (from science teacher, science catalog, or hobby store)
- small bottles of food coloring (red, yellow, green, and blue)
- clear vial with cap

1. **Ask an adult** to plug a lamp or light socket into an electrical outlet and screw in a clear tubular showcase lightbulb with a long single straight filament.
2. Add a drop of blue food coloring to a clear plastic vial. Then fill the vial with water.
3. Put a cap on the vial and gently shake.
4. Hold a diffraction grating between your eye and the light. You should see the colors spread out in a spectrum.

5. Now, hold the vial of blue solution with your other hand. Move the vial behind the grating (Figure 7). You may see that the blue pigments have absorbed some of the colors from the spectrum. Write down the colors the blue solution has removed.

6. Repeat the experiment for each of the other food colorings.

7. What colors did each food coloring remove? Were your results what you expected?

Figure 7

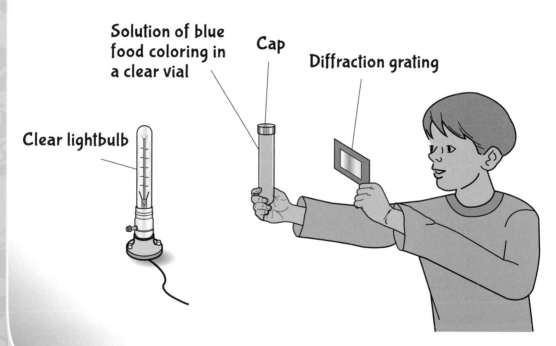

Clear lightbulb

Solution of blue food coloring in a clear vial

Cap

Diffraction grating

This experiment shows what colors of light are subtracted by different food colorings (usually red, green, blue, and yellow).

Subtracting Colored Light Using Pigments: An Explanation

The authors found and recorded the following data:

Food coloring	What colors the pigments removed	Colors that remained
blue	all the green and some red	blue and some red
green	all the blue and some red	green and some red
yellow	all the blue	green and red
red	all colors except red	red

How do your results compare with the authors' data?

Don't be surprised if your results are different. Different brands of food coloring may contain different pigments.

Experiment 10: Subtracting Colors Using Water Color Paints

Things You Will Need:

- watercolor paints
- small paintbrush
- paper
- water

You can also subtract colors using the pigments in a tablet of watercolors.

1. Wet a small paintbrush. Then use it to gather some blue paint. Spread the paint on a sheet of paper.

2. Rinse the brush in water to remove the blue paint. Then dip the brush in yellow paint.

3. Add the yellow paint to the blue paint on the paper. What color do you see when the two paints are mixed? Write down what you find.

4. Repeat the process using red and yellow paints, red and blue paints, red, blue, and yellow paints, and any other combinations you care to make.

   The authors recorded their results in the following chart. How do your results compare with theirs?

Colors mixed	Color seen in mixture
blue + yellow	green
red + yellow	reddish orange
red + blue	bluish purple
red + blue + yellow	dark, almost black

Subtracting Colored Light Using Pigments (Paint): An Explanation

The primary colors for artists—red, yellow, and blue—are really magenta, yellow, and cyan. Magenta, yellow, and cyan are the complementary colors for the primary colors of light. (See Figure 3).

It's not surprising to find that cyan and yellow pigments combine to make green. Cyan pigments would reflect blue and green light and absorb red; yellow pigments would reflect green and red light and absorb blue light. The combination would result in the reflection of green and the absorption of the other colors.

Both red (magenta) and yellow pigments reflect red light. Red (magenta) would absorb green light and reflect red and blue; yellow would absorb blue light and reflect red and green. The combination reflects primarily red.

Red (magenta) absorbs green light. It reflects blue and red light. And blue (cyan) reflects green and blue light and absorbs red. Ideally, we would expect to see blue but there are enough other pigments to darken the color, giving it a darker blue or purple color.

The combination of red (magenta), blue (cyan), and yellow was very dark. Magenta absorbs green light; cyan absorbs red light; yellow absorbs blue light. Since most of the light is absorbed, the combination is very dark.

Your results may be different. Paints differ in the kind of pigments they contain. There is often a mixture of pigments that absorb and reflect light differently. However, you can now play with your paints having more knowledge of how the pigments interact.

Artists can add and subtract colors to make beautiful landscapes that look like the real thing.

The next time you see a rainbow or a beautiful painting, you can wow your friends and family with your new knowledge of color. You can learn more about the world around you by taking a look at the other books in this series, which investigate light, sound, animals, stars, and time. Keep exploring, scientist!

GLOSSARY

afterimage—An image that continues to exist even when the stimulation producing that image ends.

color filter—A filter, usually made of colored glass or plastic, that selectively absorbs colors while letting others pass.

complementary color—Either one of two colors that when mixed produce white (in the case of light) or gray (in the case of pigments).

diffraction grating—Optical device that diffracts a beam of light to produce its spectrum.

pigment—Dry coloring matter mixed with a liquid (water, oil, etc.) to produce paint.

primary color—A color that when mixed produces other colors. Red, green, and blue are the primary colors of light because they can be mixed to produce other colors including white.

prism—Optical device made of glass or plastic used to deviate or bend a beam of light and separate it into colors.

shadow—An area of shade cast upon a surface by an object between a light source and that surface.

LEARN MORE

Books

Boothroyd, Jennifer. *Light Makes Colors*. Minneapolis, MN: Lerner Publishing Group, 2014.

DK. *Color Illusions*. London: DK Children, 2014.

Winston, Robert. *Science Rocks*. London: DK Children, 2011.

Websites

Color Matters

colormatters.com/color-and-science

This website is devoted to color, with lots of information for both adults and kids.

PBS Kids: Dragonfly TV

pbskids.org/dragonflytv/show/lightandcolor.html

This fun video explores light and color.

INDEX